DIXIE'S
FOOTBALL PRIDE

ROLL TIDE

THE MOST SPECTACULAR SIGHTS
& SOUNDS OF ALABAMA FOOTBALL

DIXIE'S FOOTBALL PRIDE

THE MOST SPECTACULAR SIGHTS
& SOUNDS OF ALABAMA FOOTBALL

Athlon® Sports™

Rutledge Hill Press™
Nashville, Tennessee

A Division of Thomas Nelson Publishers, Inc.
www.ThomasNelson.com

Published by Rutledge Hill Press, a Division of Thomas Nelson, Inc., P.O. Box 141000, Nashville, Tennessee, 37214.

1-4016-0100-6

Printed in the United States of America
03 04 05 06 07—5 4 3 2 1

TABLE of CONTENTS

ACKNOWLEDGMENTS

Athlon Sports would like to thank Rutledge Hill Press, Kevin Daniels, the College Football Hall of Fame, the University of Alabama Sports Information office, the Million Dollar Band, and above all the Bama fans, whose passionate devotion to their Crimson Tide defines what college football is all about.

INTRODUCTION

For many of us, any discussion of Southern football starts and ends with the Alabama Crimson Tide.

You may be surprised to learn, then, that the Alabama fight song mentions the Rose Bowl. Don't be. It's only fitting that there's a link between the Granddaddy of all Bowl Games and the Gold Standard of all college football programs.

You see, Alabama's rich football tradition harkens back to a time when the Rose Bowl

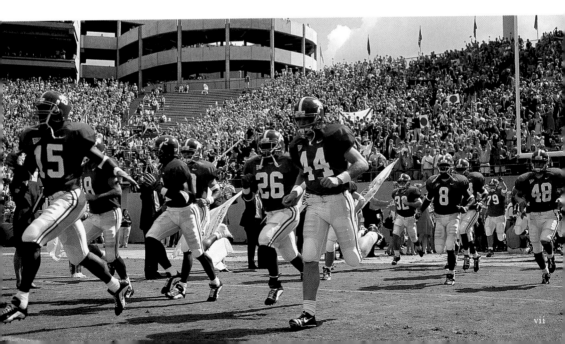

invited the best teams in the land, regardless of conference affiliation. It should be no shock that Alabama fell in that category more than once during college football's formative years.

Decades have passed, but one thing hasn't changed: Alabama Crimson Tide football is a tradition, a legacy of greatness, a virtual way of life. From the days of Wallace Wade and Frank Thomas, to the epic era of Bear Bryant, to the 1992 national championship, Alabama is synonymous with college football excellence.

AT A LOT OF PLACES, THEY JUST PLAY FOOTBALL.
AT ALABAMA, WE LIVE IT.

The Alabama media guide puts it this way:

> Summers in Alabama can be tough — hot, dry, and humid — but when the heat builds up around Tuscaloosa on a sunny August day, folks in Alabama know it's close to the kickoff of football season.

The fortunate few who arrive to begin preparations for the upcoming football season are indeed lucky. It will be those young men who will have the honor of casting their mark on one of the most storied football programs in America — Alabama.

Home to 12 national championships, 21 Southeastern Conference championships, 51 bowl appearances and the best college football coach in history, Alabama football is known and respected around the nation.

The Alabama fight song may sum it up best when it says, "Cause Bama's pluck and grit have writ her name in Crimson flame . . . Remember the Rose Bowl, we'll win then . . . you're Dixie's football pride, Crimson Tide."

At a lot of places, they just play football. At Alabama, we live it.

TRADITIONS AND PAGEANTRY

"No one can help but be aware of the rich tradition that is associated with this team and this University. Tradition is a burden in many ways. To have a tradition like ours means that you can't lose your cool; to have tradition like ours means you always have to show class, even when you are not quite up to it; to have tradition like ours means that you have to do some things that you don't want to do and some you even think you can't do, simply because tradition demands it of you. On the other hand, tradition is that which allows us to prevail in ways that we could not otherwise." — *Former Alabama President David Mathews*

I

THE CRIMSON TIDE

Lacking an official nickname, the Alabama football teams of the nineteenth century were simply referred to as "The Varsity" or "Crimson White." Soon thereafter, the nickname "The Thin Red Line" was used as an official moniker until 1907. In his write-up of that year's Alabama – Auburn game, *Birmingham Age-Herald* sportswriter Hugh Roberts coined the term "Crimson Tide" to describe Bama's style of play in a 6–6 tie with the heavily favored cross-state rival in a quagmire of red mud. *Birmingham News* sports editor Zipp Newman took the ball and ran with it, popularizing the nickname for posterity.

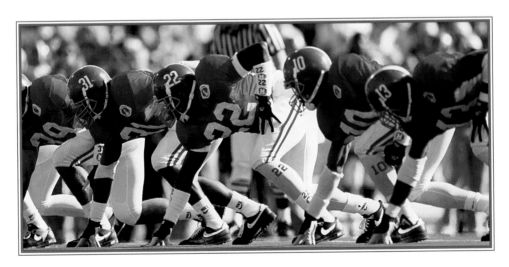

RED ELEPHANTS

Alabama's mascot, Big Al, is an elephant. Why does a team nicknamed for an oceanic phenomenon have an elephant for a mascot?

Everett Strupper was a game official for the Southern Conference and wrote a weekly column during football season for the *Atlanta Journal* about the games he officiated. Strupper worked the Alabama – Ole Miss game on October 4, 1930, when Bama coach Wallace Wade started his second team and took a first-quarter lead against the outmanned Rebels. Strupper penned these words for his newspaper's October 8 edition:

> At the end of the quarter, the earth started to tremble, there was a distant rumble that continued to grow. Some excited fan in the stands bellowed, 'Hold your horses, the elephants are coming,' and out stampeded this Alabama varsity. It was the first time that I had seen it and the size of the entire eleven nearly knocked me cold, men that I had seen play last year looking like they had nearly doubled in size.

Bama won the game 64–0 and went on to a 10–0 record and a national championship.

The pachyderm reference caught on and soon evolved into "red elephants" to include the crimson jerseys.

"THE EARTH STARTED TO TREMBLE, THERE WAS A DISTANT RUMBLE THAT CONTINUED TO GROW. SOME EXCITED FAN IN THE STANDS BELLOWED, 'HOLD YOUR HORSES, THE ELEPHANTS ARE COMING,' AND OUT STAMPEDED THIS ALABAMA VARSITY."

The Million Dollar Band

The University of Alabama Million Dollar Band is one of the sparkling gems of college football halftime tradition. More than 330 students, representing a variety of majors, comprise the group.

It began as a military band in 1914, and soon assumed its function as the centerpiece of halftime festivities under the direction of Col. Carleton K. Butler, the "Father of the Million Dollar Band." In the early days, the organization had to use all the resourcefulness at its command to raise travel funds — thus the name "Million Dollar Band" was coined in 1922 by W. C. "Champ" Pickens, an Alabama alumnus and former football manager.

ROLL TIDE

BRYANT-DENNY STADIUM

Alabama's home football stadium was christened The George Hutcheson Denny Stadium with a 55–0 victory over Mississippi College on September 28, 1929. It was officially dedicated the following week, as the Crimson Tide defeated Ole Miss 22–7. The original seating capacity was 12,000. Periodic expansion projects over the years have increased that number to its current 83,818, with plans to further expand to 93,000 within the next few years.

In 1975, the historic facility was renamed Bryant-Denny Stadium in honor of legendary coach Bear Bryant. Since its opening three-quarters of a century ago, the Crimson Tide has compiled a record of 191–37–3 within its confines.

FIGHT SONG "YEA ALABAMA"

YEA ALABAMA! DROWN 'EM TIDE,

EVERY BAMA MAN'S BEHIND YOU,

HIT YOUR STRIDE.

GO TEACH THE BULLDOGS TO BEHAVE,

SEND THE YELLOW JACKETS TO A WATERY GRAVE,

AND IF A MAN STARTS TO WEAKEN,

THAT'S A SHAME!

FOR BAMA'S PLUCK AND GRIT HAVE

WRIT HER NAME IN CRIMSON FLAME.

FIGHT ON, FIGHT ON, FIGHT ON MEN!

REMEMBER THE ROSE BOWL, WE'LL WIN THEN.

SO, ROLL ON TO VICTORY, HIT YOUR STRIDE!

YOU'RE DIXIE'S FOOTBALL PRIDE,

CRIMSON TIDE, ROLL TIDE, ROLL TIDE!

ALMA MATER

Alabama, listen, mother,
To our vows of love,
To thyself and to each other,
Faithful friends we'll prove.

Faithful, loyal, firm and true,
Heart bound to heart will beat
Year by year, the ages through,
Until in heaven we meet.

College days are swiftly fleeting,
Soon we'll leave their halls,
Ne'er to join another meeting
'Neath their hallowed walls.

Faithful, loyal, firm and true,
Heart bound to heart will beat
Year by year, the ages through,
Until in heaven we meet.

So, farewell, dear Alma Mater.
May thy name, we pray,
Be rev'renced ever, pure and stainless
As it is today.

Faithful, loyal, firm and true,
Heart bound to heart will beat
Year by year, the ages through,
Until in heaven we meet.

GREAT COACHES

If any name is synonymous with Alabama football, it is Paul William "Bear" Bryant. In 1981 Bryant surpassed Amos Alonzo Stagg's record of 314 coaching victories with Bama's win over archrival Auburn. Following the 1982 season, the Bear retired after accumulating 323 wins — a Division I-A mark that stood for two decades — at four different schools. Bryant had left Texas A&M for Alabama following the 1957 season because, in his words, "Mama called."

Bryant was a 6'3", 196-pound end for coach Frank Thomas's 1934 national champions at Alabama and was as tough a football player as ever lived. Bryant had a cast removed before the 1935 Tennessee game in order to play with a broken leg he had suffered two weeks earlier. While the "other" end on that legendary Alabama team — Don Hutson — is renowned as a receiver, Bryant was a bone-jarring blocker and an intimidating tackler.

In 25 years as Crimson Tide coach, Bryant never fielded a losing team. What was the secret of his success? "If there's one word for it, it's work," he once told a reporter. "A winning football effort demands sacrifice, discipline, oneness, and fight. That's stuff you can't learn in the classroom."

Bryant's ledger at Bama reads 232-46-9 with 24 straight bowl appearances, 13 Southeastern Conference championships and six national titles. His final game was a 21–15 win over Illinois in the Liberty Bowl on December 29, 1982. Less than a month later, he passed away at age 69. In 1986, the Bear was inducted into the College Football Hall of Fame.

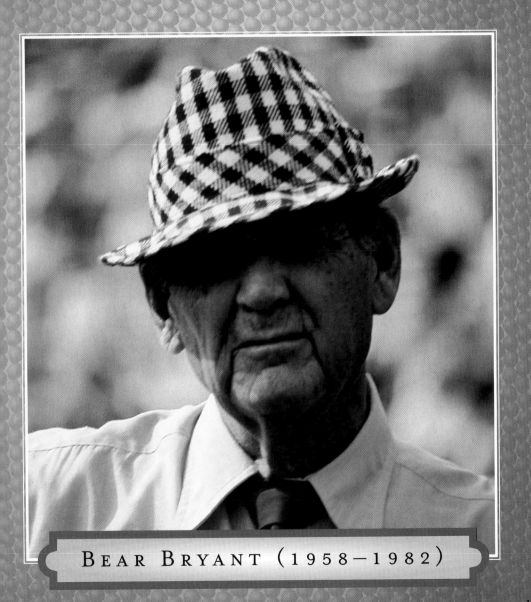

BEAR BRYANT (1958–1982)

WALLACE WADE (1923-1930)

ROLL TIDE

As head coach at Alabama, Wallace Wade compiled a record of 61-13-3. With his single-wing offense and emphasis on the kicking game, he brought three national titles to Tuscaloosa — in 1925, 1926, and 1930. Wade was too much of a perfectionist to accept defeat. He once said, "The best you can do is not good enough unless it does the job."

Wade's 1925 Bama squad was the first Southern representative in the Rose Bowl, from which the Crimson Tide came home 20-19 victors over Washington. A return trip to Pasadena ensued upon a 9-0 regular season the following year. His 1930 team may have been his best, posting a perfect 10-0 record, beating Washington State 24-0 in the Rose Bowl and winning another national championship. In 1955, Wade was enshrined in the Hall of Fame.

Frank Thomas carried on the winning ways of his predecessor, Wallace Wade. Thomas won 115 of his 146 games as Alabama's coach for a winning percentage of .812.

Thomas played quarterback at Notre Dame under Knute Rockne — George Gipp was Thomas' roommate — and enjoyed a successful stint as coach at Chattanooga before taking the Alabama job. He introduced the famous Notre Dame system of attack that he had learned from Rockne to Southern football. And with glorious results. Two of Thomas' Crimson Tide teams, in 1934 and 1941, were national champions. The 1934 unit, featuring All-Americans in halfback Dixie Howell, end Don Hutson, and tackle Bill Lee, is considered to be one of the greatest of all time.

Thomas is a charter member of the College Football Hall of Fame, inducted in the inaugural year of 1951.

FRANK THOMAS (1931-1946)

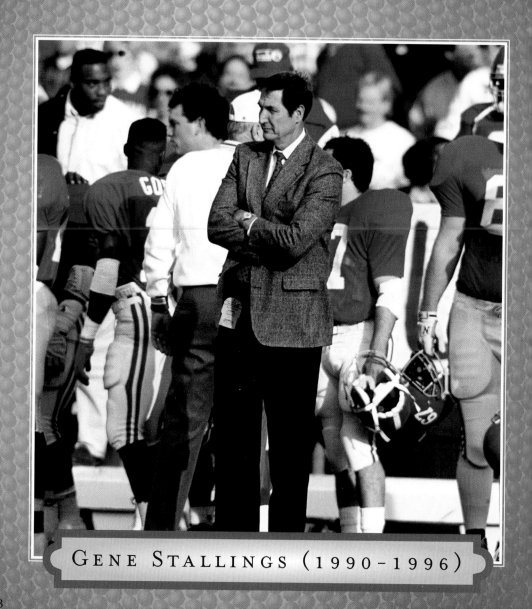

GENE STALLINGS (1990–1996)

One of the famous Junction Boys — Bear Bryant's 1954 Texas A&M team — Gene Stallings coached Alabama to a unanimous national championship in 1992. That memorable '92 campaign was capped by a rousing 34–13 rout of top-ranked Miami in the Sugar Bowl. Stallings' 1991 and '92 teams were 24–1 over those two years, including the 13–0 champs. His 62–25 ledger in Tuscaloosa included four SEC West titles and a 28–21 victory over Florida in the inaugural SEC Championship Game in 1992.

GREAT RIVALRIES

THE IRON BOWL

College football television analyst Beano Cook said it well: "Alabama — Auburn is not just a rivalry. It's Gettysburg South." According to Bill Cromartie, author of many books on college football rivalries, including *Bragging Rights*, a history of the Alabama — Auburn series: "This is by far, I think, the nastiest rivalry in the country. I doubt if anything else touches it."

Former Alabama coach Ray Perkins called it the most important football game in the world. "More people in Alabama care passionately about it than the Super Bowl," he said. He was right. Alabamians align themselves on one side against the other from the day they are born.

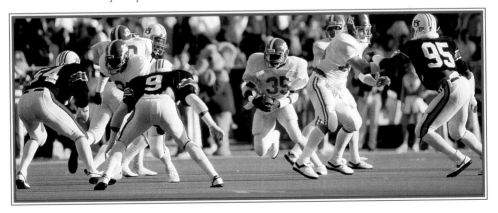

"Talk about the Texas — Texas A&M game will start a week before the game and continue for a week after," said former Alabama coach Gene Stallings, an ex-Aggie player and head coach. "But talk about the Alabama — Auburn game never stops. They're talking about it on the Fourth of July. That's what makes it different from all the others."

There's something strange about this series, though. Something else that sets it apart from other rivalries rooted in antiquity. After playing to a 6–6 tie in 1907, they didn't meet on the gridiron again until 1948, when Alabama won 55–0.

Since the first Alabama — Auburn game was played on February 22, 1893, at Lakeview Park in Birmingham, the Tide has tamed the Tigers to the tune of 38 wins, 28 losses, and a tie.

COLLEGE FOOTBALL TELEVISION ANALYST BEANO COOK SAID IT WELL: "ALABAMA–AUBURN IS NOT JUST A RIVALRY. IT'S GETTYSBURG SOUTH."

Bear Bryant's Crimson Tide teams won 19 of their 25 games against Auburn. Bama's 34–0 triumph over Auburn in 1961 was the centerpiece of the first of Bryant's six national titles. In 1971, two days after Auburn quarterback Pat Sullivan was named the winner of the Heisman Trophy, All-American Johnny Musso led a 31–7 trouncing of Auburn, with the Crimson Tide defense holding Sullivan to the lowest yardage total of his career.

Bryant's 315th career coaching victory, a 28–17 win over Auburn in 1981, made him the all-time winningest coach in Division I-A history.

In the 1985 meeting the lead changed hands four times in the fourth quarter. Van Tiffin kicked a 52-yard field goal on the last play to win it 25–23 for the Tide. In 2001, quarterback Andrew Zow and tailback Santonio Beard led the way to a 31–7 Bama win, the most lopsided final tally in the rivalry in almost a quarter-century.

The Third Saturday in October

It's not always played on that particular calendar date any more, but mention the third Saturday in October to any college football fan and the Alabama – Tennessee rivalry is what springs to mind. Alabama dominated the series in the early years of the twentieth century, ending in 1914 before a 14-year hiatus. It was resumed in 1928, during the Wallace Wade coaching era. Bama had won two national championships under Wade, in 1925 and '26, and an 18–6 win over Tennessee in 1930 helped propel the Tide to a third national title.

THE 25-0 ALABAMA VICTORY IN KNOXVILLE IN 1935 WAS HIGHLIGHTED BY THE ROUSING PLAY OF TIDE END PAUL "BEAR" BRYANT, WHO PLAYED THE GAME WITH A BROKEN LEG AND HAD A HAND IN BOTH OF BAMA'S FIRST-PERIOD TOUCHDOWNS.

Frank Thomas succeeded Wade as coach at Alabama in 1931, and the former Notre Dame quarterback quickly gained the upper hand over Tennessee. Starting in 1933, the Tide won four of the next five over the Vols, with a scoreless tie in 1936. The 1934 game in Birmingham featured Alabama's great passing tandem of halfback Dixie Howell and end Don Hutson. They combined on a long pass to set up one touchdown, and Hutson scored the other on an end-around as Alabama won 13–6.

The 25–0 Alabama victory in Knoxville in 1935 was highlighted by the rousing play of Tide end Paul "Bear" Bryant, who played the game with a broken leg and had a hand in both of Bama's first-quarter touchdowns. He caught a pass to set up one score and served as the middle man in a bit of razzle-dazzle that sent Riley Smith into the end zone for the second touchdown.

In eight of the 10 games matching Thomas against Tennessee coach Bob Neyland, both teams came in with unbeaten records. Add to these the earlier Neyland – Wade series and the wartime games, and it all adds up to 14 times in 18 meetings that both teams had gone into the third Saturday in October undefeated.

Bear Bryant had never lost to Tennessee as a player, and in 1958 he returned to his alma mater as coach. Beginning in 1961, his Tide teams reeled off four straight wins, a tie, then another win over the Vols. These were the years when Alabama resumed its old habit of winning conference and national championships.

For eleven straight meetings, 1971 through 1981, the Tide came out on top. In 1972, Bama scored two touchdowns in 36 seconds of the final two minutes to win

17–10. Former Alabama end and then-Tennessee coach Bill Battle's teams had lost six in a row to Bryant when he was replaced by John Majors, whose teams lost five straight to the Bear. Bryant's Alabama scorecard against the Vols was 16–7–2.

In 1986, under coach Ray Perkins, Alabama scored more points than either team ever had in the series, winning 56–28. That '86 contest began a nine-year unbeaten streak against the Volunteers, with a 17–17 tie in 1993. Coach Gene Stallings and the Tide were defending a national title in '93, when Stallings put flanker David Palmer in the Tennessee game at quarterback for some fourth-quarter heroics. Palmer ran for a touchdown, then circled right end on another run with 21 seconds left for the two-point conversion and the tie.

No program had ever beaten Alabama seven straight times until Tennessee accomplished the feat from 1995-2001. But in the 2002 game, Alabama forced six Tennessee turnovers on the way to a resounding 34–14 triumph, and in a series characterized by streaks, the '02 victory is an encouraging omen for the Tide faithful.

THE CHAMPIONSHIPS

There are almost too many national championships to fully elaborate on them all. According to the NCAA official records, Alabama has won at least part of seventeen national titles, six of them of the consensus variety. Two of those, in 1979 and 1992, were unanimous. And though Minnesota garnered the lion's share of the national championship recognition in 1934, coach Frank Thomas' Crimson Tide that year was undeniably one of the greatest college football teams ever fielded. Bama also shared national titles with Michigan State in 1965, with Notre Dame in '73, and with USC in '78. And in 1966, an 11–0 Crimson Tide finished third in both polls behind Notre Dame and Michigan State, who had played each other to a tie.

Here's a quick look at the best of the best:

1 9 3 4 (1 0 – 0)

It's a shame Minnesota didn't have to play Alabama in 1934, or the national title picture that season might have had a Crimson tint to it. This was unquestionably one of the greatest football teams of all-time. With Frank Thomas in his fourth year at the helm in Tuscaloosa, the Tide finished the season with a perfect 10–0 work-sheet, including a dominating 29–13 Rose Bowl win over Stanford. Halfback Dixie Howell, end Don Hutson, and tackle Bill Lee were All-Americans, headlining a star-studded lineup that also included quarterback Riley Smith, end Paul Bryant,

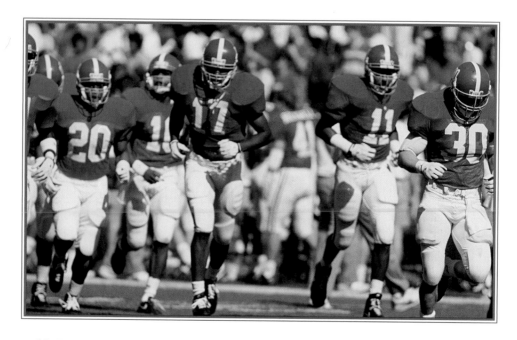

tackle Jim Whatley, and guards Arthur "Tarzan" White and Charlie Marr. Hutson
led Bama to a 13–6 victory over previously unbeaten Tennessee, and the Tide
finished the regular season with three straight shutouts — 40–0 over Clemson,
40–0 over Georgia Tech and 34–0 over Vanderbilt — to punch its ticket to Pasadena.

1 9 6 1 (1 1 — 0)

In 1961, Alabama outscored its opponents 297–25 and finished 11–0, including
five straight shutouts to end the regular season, to give Bear Bryant the first of his
six national championships. The unflappable Pat Trammell piloted the offense at
quarterback, with All-America tackle Billy Neighbors paving the way. Lee Roy

Jordan, one of the game's all-time great linebackers, put teeth in the Tide defense. A 34–0 rout of Auburn sent the Tide to New Orleans for the holidays, where Trammell's 12-yard first-quarter touchdown run was all the scoring Bama needed in its 10–3 Sugar Bowl win over Arkansas.

THERE ARE ALMOST TOO MANY NATIONAL CHAMPIONSHIPS TO FULLY ELABORATE ON THEM ALL.

1 9 6 4 (1 0 − 1)

Quarterback Joe Namath led the 1964 Crimson Tide to a 10–0 regular season and yet another national championship. Namath scored three touchdowns in a 31–3 season-opening win over Georgia. In Game 4, a 21–0 win over NC State, Namath suffered a knee injury that would dog him throughout his career. On November 7 in Birmingham, Bryant had put in an order for dry conditions to aid in his team's effort against unbeaten LSU. During pregame warm-ups, the field was wet and rain was falling — until the Bear emerged from the tunnel. At that moment, the rain relented and the sun came out, and Alabama beat the Bayou Bengals 17–9. A 21–14 win over Auburn sealed a perfect regular season. Namath's fourth-quarter touchdown on a six-inch sneak that would have beaten Texas in the Orange Bowl was ruled short, though one official and Namath's teammates saw him score. The final score stood 21–17 Texas, but Bama had been awarded the title by both the AP and UPI.

1 9 6 5 (9 − 1 − 1)

Despite a season-opening one-point loss to Georgia and a rare red-zone blunder by Kenny Stabler, subbing for an injured Steve Sloan, that led to a 7–7 tie with

Tennessee, Alabama captured the Associated Press portion of the 1965 national title. Sloan's heroics in overcoming a 16-7 fourth-quarter deficit against Ole Miss to win 17–16 kept the Tide's title hopes alive. Alabama added emphasis to the '65 campaign by routing Auburn 30–3 to conclude the regular season. Bryant's club then proceeded to overwhelm a big, bulky 10–0 Nebraska team with speed and quickness in the Orange Bowl. Ray Perkins was on the receiving end of two Sloan touchdown passes in the 39–28 victory over the Cornhuskers that wasn't as close as the score indicated.

1 9 7 8 (1 1 − 1)

Alabama entered the 1978 season as the No. 1 team in the nation. The Crimson Tide avenged the previous season's loss to Nebraska — the only smudge on an otherwise perfect record — by whipping the Huskers 20–3 to open the campaign. Then the Tide hit a speed bump in Game 3 with a 24–14 loss to USC in the L.A. Coliseum. But Bear Bryant's men would not be deterred. They captured their seventh SEC crown in eight years with a 7–0 league mark, accented by a 34–16 victory over Auburn. By this time Bama had climbed back to No. 2 in the polls; Penn State was No. 1. The Sugar Bowl would decide the issue. Bama prevailed over the Nittany Lions 14–7 in a game for the ages. The most famous goal-line stand in history, with All-American Barry Krauss making the most famous tackle in Alabama history, preserved the win — and the national title in the AP poll.

1 9 7 9 (1 2 − 0)

After sharing the title with Southern Cal in 1978, Bryant's 1979 squad took on all comers on the way to a 12–0 record and a No. 1 final ranking in both polls. All-America offensive linemen Dwight Stephenson and Jim Bunch led the way for quarterback Steadman Shealy and halfback Major Ogilvie as the Tide racked up

383 points to 67 for its opponents. End E. J. Junior, linebacker Thomas Boyd, and cornerback Don McNeal solidified the defense. The only close call all year was a 3–0 win at LSU. Ogilvie took Sugar Bowl MVP honors, notching a pair of touchdown runs and returning a punt 50 yards to set up a field goal in a 24–9 triumph over Arkansas.

1 9 9 2 (1 3 – 0)

Alabama celebrated its football centennial with a national championship. Gene Stallings, a former Bryant player and assistant, was now in command in Tuscaloosa. Sophomore Jay Barker took over at quarterback to start the season and would end his career as the winningest signal-caller in school history. But it was defense that separated this team from the rest of the pack. Antonio Langham and George Teague both picked off six passes that year. Langham and defensive linemen John Copeland and Eric Curry were All-Americans. The Tide tamed the Tigers in the Iron Bowl, disposed of the Florida Gators in the first-ever SEC Championship Game, and handed the Miami Hurricanes their heads on a platter in a 34–13 Sugar Bowl triumph.

GREAT PLAYERS

ALABAMA IN THE COLLEGE FOOTBALL HALL OF FAME

POOLEY HUBERT (QUARTERBACK, 1922–25)
INDUCTED 1964

Pooley Hubert quarterbacked Alabama to its first postseason appearance ever — a 20–19 win over Washington in the 1926 Rose Bowl. In his four years as a letterman Hubert scored 38 touchdowns for Alabama. He scored at least three times in each of six different games. He was All-Southern two years and All-America as a senior.

JOHNNY MACK BROWN (HALFBACK, 1923–25)
INDUCTED 1957

Johnny Mack Brown was a hit as a cowboy in Hollywood Westerns, but he was an even bigger hit as a football player. The "Dothan Antelope" ran with a reckless abandon that terrorized opponents. During his three years with the varsity, the Tide went 25–3–1, including the perfect 10–0 national championship campaign in 1925.

FRED SINGTON (TACKLE, 1928–30)

INDUCTED 1955

Fred Sington was All-Southern, All-America, Phi Beta Kappa, and student body vice-president. He won all the scholastic and athletic awards the University of Alabama had to give his senior year. He was a leader of Wallace Wade's 1930 national and Rose Bowl champions. Notre Dame coach Knute Rockne called Sington "the greatest lineman in the country."

JOHNNY CAIN (FULLBACK, 1930–32)

INDUCTED 1973

Johnny "Hurri" Cain was a two-time All-American and three-time All-Southern. Cain's most famous game came as a punter, when he dueled Tennessee's Beattie Feathers in the rain and mud of Legion Field in 1932. Cain averaged 48 yards on 19 punts that day.

DIXIE HOWELL (HALFBACK, 1932–34)

INDUCTED 1970

The throwing component of the deadly Howell-to-Hutson passing combo, Millard F. "Dixie" Howell led the Crimson Tide to the national championship in his All-America senior season of 1934. Howell's performance in a 29–13 victory over Stanford in the 1935 Rose Bowl was unforgettable. He passed for 160 yards, rushed for 111, and averaged 44 yards on six punts. Famed sportswriter Grantland Rice wrote this:

"Dixie Howell, the 161-pound human howitzer from Hartford, Alabama, blasted the Rose Bowl dreams of Stanford today with one of the greatest all-around exhibitions football has ever known."

DON HUTSON (END, 1932–34)

INDUCTED 1951

In the 1935 Rose Bowl, Don Hutson caught six passes for 165 yards, including 59- and 54-yard touchdowns. Tall, fluid, and fast, Hutson was arguably the greatest pass-catcher of the first half of the 20th century. Frank Thomas called Hutson "the best player I ever coached." Hutson is a charter member of the College Football Hall of Fame, and after making All-Pro nine times and League MVP twice during his 11-year NFL career with the Green Bay Packers, he also has a shrine in his honor in the Pro Football Hall of Fame.

RILEY SMITH (QUARTERBACK, 1933–35)

INDUCTED 1985

The quarterback of Frank Thomas' 1934 juggernaut was Riley Smith, who had switched from fullback after the 1933 season. In 1935, Smith was an All-American. He was also a recipient of the Jacobs Award as the Southeastern Conference's best blocker.

DON WHITMIRE (TACKLE, 1941–42)

INDUCTED 1956

Tackle Don Whitmire split his college career between Alabama (1941-42) and the Naval Academy (1943-44). His career in the Navy saw him advance to the rank of admiral. Whitmire was a 6'2", 220-pound blocker and tackler who hit like a truck.

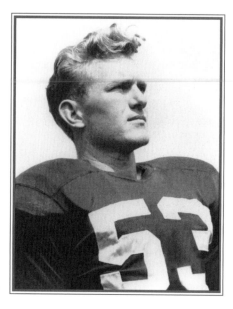

HARRY GILMER (QUARTERBACK, 1944–47)

INDUCTED 1993

Harry Gilmer scored more touchdowns — 50 — than any other player in Alabama's storied football history. He was an All-American and SEC Player of the Year in 1945, and he concluded that season as Rose Bowl MVP in Bama's 34–14 win over USC. In 1946 he led the Crimson Tide in rushing, passing, interceptions, punt returns, and kickoff returns. His 436 punt-return yards in 1946 still stand as the school single-season record.

VAUGHN MANCHA (CENTER, 1944–47)

INDUCTED 1990

Vaughn Mancha was Alabama's starting center for four full seasons, beginning with the first game of his freshman year. Frank Thomas' 1945 Tide went 10–0 and beat USC in the Rose Bowl with Mancha as an All-American.

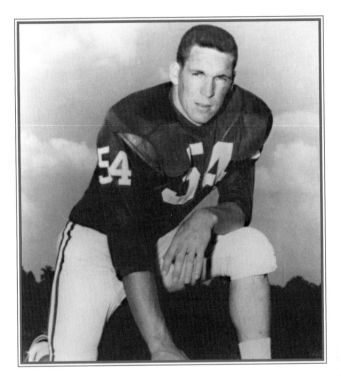

LEE ROY JORDAN (LINEBACKER, 1960–62)

INDUCTED 1983

"If they stay inside the boundaries," Bear Bryant once said, "Lee Roy will get 'em." Jordan made 31 tackles in his last college game, a 17–0 Bama win over Oklahoma in the 1963 Orange Bowl. He was an All-American and fourth-highest Heisman Trophy vote-getter in 1962, was voted Alabama's Player of the Decade for the 1960s, and is a member of both the College Football Hall of Fame and the Dallas Cowboys' Ring of Honor.

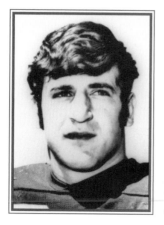

JOHNNY MUSSO (HALFBACK, 1969–71)

INDUCTED 2000

When Bear Bryant unveiled Alabama's wishbone offense in 1971, senior halfback Johnny Musso was called upon to carry the load. Musso, the "Italian Stallion," was a two-year All-American and a unanimous choice as a senior, when he came in fourth in the Heisman Trophy balloting. He was also an Academic All-American and the 1971 SEC Player of the Year.

JOHN HANNAH (GUARD, 1970–72)

INDUCTED 1999

If John Hannah isn't the best offensive lineman ever to play the game, he's certainly on the short list. Hannah was a two-time All-American for Bear Bryant's teams during the early 1970s, and he won the Jacobs Trophy as the Southeastern Conference's best blocker in 1972. He is a member of Alabama's All-Century Team, the Alabama Sports Hall of Fame, and both the College and Pro Football Halls of Fame.

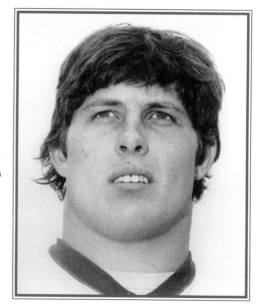

OZZIE NEWSOME (SPLIT END, 1974–77)

INDUCTED 1994

Ozzie Newsome started 47 consecutive games for the Tide and caught 102 balls for 2,070 yards, an average of 20.3 yards per reception. Newsome was instrumental in bringing three SEC titles to Tuscaloosa. He was voted Alabama's Player of the Decade for the 1970s.

OTHER BAMA GREATS

PAT TRAMMELL (QUARTERBACK, 1959–61)

Bear Bryant on Pat Trammell: "As a quarterback he had no ability. As a leader I've never had another like him." Trammell quarterbacked Alabama to the 1961 national championship, the first of six under Bryant. After leading the Tide to a 10–0 regular season in '61, Trammell scored the only touchdown on a 12-yard run in the 10–3 Sugar Bowl win over Arkansas. Trammell passed away of a brain tumor at age 28.

JOE NAMATH (QUARTERBACK, 1962–64)

As a sophomore in 1962, Joe Namath took the quarterback reins from Trammell and succeeded to the tune of a 10–1 record, including a 17–0 win over Oklahoma in the Orange Bowl. Namath quarterbacked Alabama to a 29–4 record over his three years, and in 1964 he played through a knee injury to lead the Crimson Tide to a national title. He was MVP of the 1965 Orange Bowl and Super Bowl III as quarterback of the New York Jets.

STEVE SLOAN (QUARTERBACK, 1963–65)

Steve Sloan came of age as a quarterback on Oct. 2, 1965. With his 1–1 Alabama team trailing Ole Miss 16–10 with five minutes to play, Sloan engineered a game-winning 89-yard drive and took it in for the score himself. He was an All-American that year, leading the nation in pass efficiency. He finished 10th in the 1965 Heisman voting and closed his career as MVP of the 39–28 Bama win over Nebraska in the 1966 Orange Bowl.

KENNY STABLER (QUARTERBACK, 1965–67)

In 1966, Kenny Stabler guided one of the all-time great Alabama teams to a 10–0 regular-season record, and followed that up with an MVP performance in the Tide's 34–7 Sugar Bowl win over Nebraska. As a senior the following year, he was an All-American and SEC Player of the Year. Stabler went on to enjoy a stellar career in the NFL with Oakland, Houston, and New Orleans.

CORNELIUS BENNETT (LINEBACKER, 1983–86)

Cornelius Bennett was a three-time All-America linebacker for Bama from 1984–1986. As a senior, Bennett was chosen SEC Player of the Year, won the Lombardi Award, and finished seventh in the Heisman balloting. He was Defensive Player of the Game in two different bowl games, was SEC Player of the Year in 1986, is a member of Alabama's All-Century team, and was named the school's Player of the Decade for the 1980s.

DERRICK THOMAS (LINEBACKER, 1985–88)

In 1988, Derrick Thomas compiled 27 sacks — that's in one season! His career total was an equally imposing 52. As a senior, Thomas became the first SEC player to win the Butkus Award as the nation's top linebacker. In 1989, playing for the Kansas City Chiefs, he was named NFL Rookie of the Year. Tragically, Thomas lost his life on February 8, 2000 due to injuries sustained in an auto accident.

JAY BARKER (QUARTERBACK, 1991–94)

Jay Barker finished his career in 1994 as Alabama's all-time passing leader, capturing the Johnny Unitas Golden Arm Award as a senior. Barker established eight school career records, quarterbacked the Crimson Tide to the 1992 national championship as a sophomore, and posted a 34–2–1 record as a starter, making him the winningest quarterback in Alabama history.

SHAUN ALEXANDER (TAILBACK, 1996–99)

Shaun Alexander ran for more yards (3,565) than anyone else in Alabama history. His game at LSU as a freshman, when he ran for 291 yards on 20 carries, is unforgettable. It is also a school record. As a senior in 1999, Alexander rushed for 1,383 yards and 19 touchdowns, finished seventh in the Heisman voting, was named SEC Player of the Year, and was an All-American.

CHRIS SAMUELS (OFFENSIVE TACKLE, 1996–99)

Offensive tackle Chris Samuels brought the Outland Trophy to Tuscaloosa in 1999. He also won the Jacobs Award as the best blocker in the Southeastern Conference. That season he allowed opposing defenders zero sacks and zero pressures. He started 42 consecutive games during his Alabama career and was the third overall pick in the 2000 NFL Draft.

TALKIN' BAMA FOOTBALL

"I'll never forget going to the Rose Bowl. I remember everything about it. We were on the train and coach (Frank) Thomas was talking to three coaches and Red Heard, the athletic director at LSU. Coach Thomas said, 'Red, this is my best football player. This is the best player on my team.' Well shoot, I could have gone right out the top. He was getting me ready and I was, too. I would have gone out there and killed myself for Alabama that day."

BEAR BRYANT, ON BAMA'S 1935 ROSE BOWL TRIP.

"I thought this must be what God looks like."

HALL-OF-FAMER GEORGE BLANDA, ABOUT HIS FIRST ENCOUNTER WITH BEAR BRYANT.

"I know one thing, I'd rather die now than to have died this morning and missed this game."

THE BEAR AFTER BAMA'S WIN OVER UNBEATEN AUBURN IN '71.

"You'd better pass."

"I can't imagine being in the Hall of Fame with Coach Bryant. There ought to be two Halls of Fame, one for Coach Bryant and one for everybody else."

"HE LITERALLY KNOCKED THE DOOR DOWN.

I mean, right off the hinges. A policeman came in and asked who knocked the door down, and Coach Bryant said, 'I did.' The cop just said 'Okay' and walked away."

JERRY DUNCAN, DESCRIBING AN IRATE BEAR AFTER A 7–7 TIE WITH TENNESSEE.

"I wish Coach Bryant were here to see this defense play."

DEFENSIVE COORDINATOR BILL OLIVER
ABOUT THE '92 NATIONAL CHAMPIONSHIP DEFENSE.

"In the second quarter, I saw (Gino) Torretta look over at me and he froze for a second. **I SAW FEAR.**"

BAMA DEFENSIVE END JOHN COPELAND, FOLLOWING THE TIDE'S STUNNING 34–13 WINOVER MIAMI FOR THE NATIONAL CHAMPIONSHIP IN WHICH THEY SHUT DOWN HEISMAN TROPHY WINNER TORRETTA.

"You never know what a football player is made of until he plays against Alabama."

TENNESSEE COACH BOB NEYLAND.

BOWL GAME TRADITION

Alabama has played in and won more bowl games than any other college football program. In fifty-one postseason appearances, the Crimson Tide has emerged victorious from 29 of them.

1926 Rose Bowl	Alabama 20, Washington 19
1927 Rose Bowl	Alabama 7, Stanford 7
1931 Rose Bowl	Alabama 24, Washington State 0
1935 Rose Bowl	Alabama 29, Stanford 13
1938 Rose Bowl	California 13, Alabama 0
1942 Cotton Bowl	Alabama 29, Texas A&M 21
1943 Orange Bowl	Alabama 37, Boston College 21
1945 Sugar Bowl	Duke 29, Alabama 26
1946 Rose Bowl	Alabama 34, Southern Cal 14
1948 Sugar Bowl	Texas 27, Alabama 7
1953 Orange Bowl	Alabama 61, Syracuse 6
1954 Cotton Bowl	Rice 28, Alabama 6
1959 Liberty Bowl	Penn State 7, Alabama 0

1960 Bluebonnet Bowl	Alabama 3, Texas 3
1962 Sugar Bowl	Alabama 10, Arkansas 3
1963 Orange Bowl	Alabama 17, Oklahoma 0
1964 Sugar Bowl	Alabama 12, Ole Miss 7
1965 Orange Bowl	Texas 21, Alabama 17
1966 Orange Bowl	Alabama 39, Nebraska 28
1967 Sugar Bowl	Alabama 34, Nebraska 7
1968 Cotton Bowl	Texas A&M 20, Alabama 16
1968 Gator Bowl	Missouri 35, Alabama 10
1969 Liberty Bowl	Colorado 47, Alabama 33
1970 Bluebonnet Bowl	Alabama 24, Oklahoma 24
1972 Orange Bowl	Nebraska 38, Alabama 6
1973 Cotton Bowl	Texas 17, Alabama 13
1973 Sugar Bowl	Notre Dame 24, Alabama 23
1975 Orange Bowl	Notre Dame 13, Alabama 11
1975 Sugar Bowl	Alabama 13, Penn State 6
1976 Liberty Bowl	Alabama 36, UCLA 6
1978 Sugar Bowl	Alabama 35, Ohio State 6
1979 Sugar Bowl	Alabama 14, Penn State 7
1980 Sugar Bowl	Alabama 24, Arkansas 9

1981 Cotton Bowl	Alabama 30, Baylor 2
1982 Cotton Bowl	Texas 14, Alabama 12
1982 Liberty Bowl	Alabama 21, Illinois 15
1983 Sun Bowl	Alabama 28, SMU 7
1985 Aloha Bowl	Alabama 24, Southern Cal 3
1986 Sun Bowl	Alabama 28, Washington 6
1988 Hall of Fame Bowl	Michigan 28, Alabama 24
1988 Sun Bowl	Alabama 29, Army 28
1990 Sugar Bowl	Miami 33, Alabama 25
1991 Fiesta Bowl	Louisville 34, Alabama 7

1991 Blockbuster Bowl	Alabama 30, Colorado 25
1993 Sugar Bowl	Alabama 34, Miami 13
1993 Gator Bowl	Alabama 24, North Carolina 10
1995 Citrus Bowl	Alabama 24, Ohio State 17
1997 Outback Bowl	Alabama 17, Michigan 14
1998 Music City Bowl	Virginia Tech 38, Alabama 7
2000 Orange Bowl	Michigan 35, Alabama 34
2001 Independence Bowl	Alabama 14, Iowa State 13

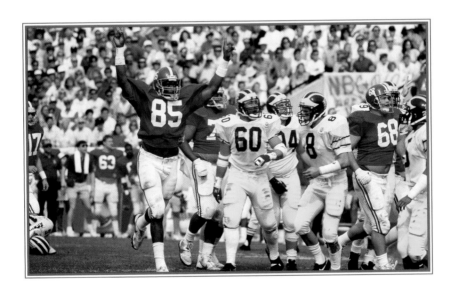

1926 ROSE BOWL

ALABAMA 20, WASHINGTON 19

Consensus opinion had Washington as the nation's best team. When Alabama accepted a bid to take on the Huskies in the Rose Bowl, sportswriters scoffed at the Tide's chances. When Coach Wallace Wade's Crimson Tide emerged from the contest a 20–19 victor, the world was aware of a new phenomenon — Southern football. Trailing 12–0 at the half, Bama knocked Washington's All-America halfback George Wilson out of the game in the third quarter and quickly took advantage, scoring three touchdowns in less than seven minutes. Pooley Hubert and Johnny Mack Brown wowed the 45,000 fans in attendance and inspired Grantland Rice-esque hyperbole in the next day's sports pages.

1935 ROSE BOWL
ALABAMA 29, STANFORD 13

Coach Frank Thomas took one of the greatest football teams of all time to Pasadena for a meeting with unbeaten Stanford. The Indians led 7–0 after the first quarter, then the immortal pass-catch combo of Dixie Howell and Don Hutson went to work. They ignited a 256-yard, 22-point second quarter that put Stanford on the mat for good. Hutson caught touchdown passes of 54 and 59 yards, and Howell scored on a 67-yard run and a five-yard run. Stanford had no answer for Bama's speed.

1946 ROSE BOWL
ALABAMA 34, USC 14

Alabama's sixth and last trip to the Rose Bowl, on New Year's Day, 1946, ended with the mighty Trojans vanquished by a score of 34–14. With All-America quarterback Harry Gilmer spearheading the attack, the Tide built a 20–0 halftime lead and never looked back. Bama led 27–0 in the third quarter before USC managed as much as a first down. Coach Frank Thomas' team outgained the Trojans 351 yards to 41. It was USC's ninth Rose Bowl appearance — and its first loss. Alabama closed the book on its New Year's Day in Pasadena tradition at 4–1–1.

1953 ORANGE BOWL

ALABAMA 61, SYRACUSE 6

Alabama set an Orange Bowl record of 586 total yards — 286 on the ground, 300 through the air—in its 61–6 demolition of Syracuse, the champions of the East, in the 1953 Orange Bowl. The Tide led 7–6 after one quarter and 21–6 at intermission. Then in the second half, the floodgates flew open, with coach Red Drew's Tide scoring 20 points in both the third and fourth periods. "I just couldn't stop them," Drew remarked.

1963 ORANGE BOWL

ALABAMA 17, OKLAHOMA 0

President John F. Kennedy was in attendance to see sophomore quarterback Joe Namath work his magic in the 1963 Orange Bowl. Namath's deft ball-handling and his 25-yard touchdown pass to end Dick Williamson sparked Alabama to a 17–0 win over Oklahoma. Bama's defense stifled the Sooner attack all day, with linebacker Lee Roy Jordan compiling an unheard-of 31 tackles.

1966 ORANGE BOWL

ALABAMA 39, NEBRASKA 28

Alabama parlayed a dominating performance over undefeated Nebraska in Miami on January 1, 1966, into a repeat national championship. Bama's speed and quickness were just too much for the Huskers to handle as Bama won 39–28. And it wasn't that close. The Tide ran twice as many plays and outgained the Cornhuskers by 141 yards in the one-sided affair. Steve Sloan connected with receiver Ray Perkins on two scoring tosses.

1967 SUGAR BOWL

ALABAMA 34, NEBRASKA 7

In a rematch of the previous season's Orange Bowl, Alabama made an even more emphatic statement than before, mugging coach Bob Devaney's Cornhuskers by a score of 34–7. The Tide rolled in at 10–0; Nebraska had been beaten once — by one point (10–9 at Oklahoma) in the season finale. Bama's first play from scrimmage was a 45-yard pass completion from Kenny Stabler to Ray Perkins. Seven plays later, Les Kelly rammed in from the one. The Tide led 17–0 after the first quarter, and the issue was never in doubt. "This was the greatest college team I've ever seen," were Bear Bryant's words. But his 11–0 squad finished third in both polls behind Notre Dame and Michigan State, who had played each other to a tie in November.

1979 SUGAR BOWL
ALABAMA 14, PENN STATE 7

The 1979 Sugar Bowl was the stage for the most memorable goal-line stand in college football history. The second-ranked Crimson Tide had broken a scoreless tie with top-ranked Penn State on a 30-yard Jeff Rutledge-to-Bruce Bolton touchdown pass with eight seconds left before intermission. Each team added a TD in the third quarter. In the fourth quarter, the Nittany Lions faced third and goal from the one yard line. Matt Suhey was stopped six inches short, and on fourth down All-America linebacker Barry Krauss met Mike Guman head-on for no gain, sealing the win and another national title for the Crimson Tide.

1993 SUGAR BOWL
ALABAMA 34, MIAMI 13

The similarities to the 1979 Sugar Bowl were striking. The host city was New Orleans. Second-ranked Alabama beat the nation's No. 1 team to claim the national championship. But there was one big difference — in the '93 Classic, Bama romped. The Tide took a 13–6 halftime lead which snowballed from there to a 34–13 rout. Coach Gene Stallings' club scored two third-quarter touchdowns in 16 seconds, the second on a 31-yard interception return by George Teague. Bama kept Hurricane Heisman Trophy-winning quarterback Gino Torretta on his heels all night, outrushed Miami 267 yards to 48 and came home with another national title.